What is Terrorism?

by the same author

Supporting Traumatized Children and Teenagers
A Guide to Providing Understanding and Help
Atle Dyregrov
ISBN 978 1 84905 034 0
ISBN 978 1 84985 660 7 (large print)
eISBN 978 0 85700 391 1

Grief in Young Children
A Handbook for Adults
Atle Dyregrov
ISBN 978 1 84310 650 0
ISBN 978 1 84985 601 0 (large print)
eISBN 978 1 84642 779 4

Grief in Children
A Handbook for Adults, Second Edition
Atle Dyregrov
ISBN 978 1 84310 612 8
eISBN 978 1 84642 781 7

Effective Grief and Bereavement Support
The Role of Family, Friends, Colleagues,
Schools and Support Professionals
Kari Dyregrov and Atle Dyregrov
ISBN 978 1 84310 667 8
eISBN 978 1 84642 833 3

of related interest

Is Daddy Coming Back in a Minute?
Explaining (sudden) death in words very
young children can understand
Elke Barber and Alex Barber
Illustrated by Anna Jarvis
ISBN 978 1 78592 106 3
eISBN 978 1 78450 371 0

I Have a Question about Death
A Book for Children with Autism Spectrum
Disorder or Other Special Needs
Arlen Grad Gaines and Meredith Englander Polsky
ISBN 978 1 78592 750 8
eISBN 978 1 78450 545 5

What is Terrorism?

A Book to Help Parents, Teachers and Other Grown-ups Talk with Kids about Terror

Atle Dyregrov, Magne Raundalen
and William Yule

Illustrated by David O'Connell

Jessica Kingsley *Publishers*
London and Philadelphia

First published in 2019
by Jessica Kingsley Publishers
73 Collier Street
London N1 9BE, UK
and
400 Market Street, Suite 400
Philadelphia, PA 19106, USA

www.jkp.com

Library of Congress Cataloging in Publication Data
Names: Dyregrov, Atle, author. | Raundalen, Magne, author. |
Yule, William, author.
Title: What is terrorism? : a book to help parents, teachers and other
grown-ups talk with kids about terror /
Atle Dyregrov, Magne Raundalen and William Yule.
Description: Philadelphia : Jessica Kingsley
Publishers, [2018] | Audience: Age: 7-12.
Identifiers: LCCN 2018008733 | ISBN 9781785924736
Subjects: LCSH: Terrorism--Juvenile literature, |
Terrorism--Prevention--Juvenile literature. | Parenting--Juvenile
literature. | Parent and child--Juvenile literature.
Classification: LCC HV6431 .D967 2018 | DDC 363.325--dc23 LC
record available at https://catalog.loc.gov/vwebv/
search?searchCode=LCCN&searchArg=2018008733
&searchType=1&permalink=y

British Library Cataloguing in Publication Data
A CIP catalogue record for this book is available from the British Library

ISBN 978 1 78592 473 6
eISBN 978 1 78450 865 4

Printed and bound in Great Britain

Contents

Preface

WHO ARE WE?

Two of us were children during the Second World War and one of us was born a few years after that war. All three of us are psychologists who've worked for many years with children who've experienced war and terror. We've worked with UNICEF and other organisations to improve the situation for children and families who experience such frightening events. We've written many books and manuals that support adults in understanding how children react to war and war-like events, and how to help them cope with what they've experienced.

We've tried to understand how terror makes children think and feel, and to find ways of explaining terror and terrorists to children.

OUR BOOK

In this book, we'll try to help you understand what terrorism is, what makes terrorists do what they do, and what you can do to prevent such acts. We'll also tell you a little about how we support children and families who are personally affected by terrorist acts.

The book is divided into two parts. You can read the first part with a child or children. The second part is for adults, and provides background and guidance about the ways you can approach conversations about terrorism with children aged seven and upwards. In this book we define 'terrorism' as something that goes on separate to war, and is perpetrated by those who kill innocent people who don't have weapons. In the second part of the book (see pages 62–66), we explain our reasons for defining terrorism the way we do and give tips and advice about ways to talk with your child about terrorism.

Part 1

· · · · ·

What is
Terrorism?

What is terror and terrorism?

You'll already be aware that sometimes you feel afraid or scared. That's perfectly normal. Occasionally, if you feel very, very scared, you might say you're 'terrified'. You can see where the word 'terrorist' comes from. In a way, terrorists are similar to bullies; they want you to fear them and obey them. A bully tries to scare or terrorise you into doing something they want you to do, even though you don't want to do it. They want to force people to do what they want. So terrorists are really just big bullies. All schools have programmes to stop bullying because it can be very harmful for children.

But terrorism tends to be more complicated than bullying, because it affects whole nations. Perhaps some people who live in a country don't like the way things are run. They feel their views and needs are ignored. When they can't get their government to listen to them, they start to fight for what they consider to be their freedoms and beliefs. They threaten to do bad things.

They bomb buildings. They shoot at crowds – anything to force the government to give in to their demands. They see themselves as 'freedom fighters'. But the government sees them as 'terrorists'.

Nowadays, the word 'terrorist' usually means someone who will use threats and killing to get their own way. They may disagree with the government over the way their group is treated; they may have a firm belief that there's only one way to do things and that any other way is wrong. If you've ever heard of *Gulliver's Travels*, you'll know that in that story two groups start fighting because one group thought that they could only open a boiled egg by smashing the shell with a spoon, while the other group thought that the only way to do it was to slice the top off with a knife! To many people, the arguments between different religious groups can seem equally silly. If only the groups didn't start killing each other.

Sometimes, countries go to war when they can't agree about things like land and resources. They train soldiers to fight, defend and kill. In these cases, we say that they're fighting for power. Usually, this sort of aggression isn't called terrorism. As we said above, terrorism is when force is used to scare people into doing things they don't want to do. That sort of terrorism has been around for hundreds of years. Many countries gained their independence by terrorising faraway countries until they gave in. In the Middle Ages, there were wars between Christians and Muslims. The Muslim empire covered most countries around the Mediterranean, but the Crusaders fought their way to Jerusalem. Sadly, these sorts of fights still happen in the Middle East.

· ·

The difference between war and terrorism

A conversation between an 11-year-old girl, Annie, and her great-grandmother, Shelly, who's nearly 90 years old

Annie: Great-grandma, you were born in 1929, and you were ten years old when war broke out and the Second World War began. Was it terrible?

Shelly: Yes, Annie, it was terrible – war and violence are the worst things that can happen to people. I was sent to a family out of London for four months when the worst bombing started.

Annie: Did you know them?

Shelly: No, I didn't, but they were very kind, and we all had to help each other, especially to protect the children from all the horror of war. But you said you had a question my dear?

Annie: Yes, I wondered about the difference between war and the terrorism that we're experiencing now. We're going to talk about it in class tomorrow and I promised to talk to an old person!

Shelly: Yes, I'm old enough for that! And I can tell you that many of my worst memories of the war have come back to me after seeing the TV reports of terror acts around Europe in the last few years and months. But there are big differences between war and terror.

Annie: But war is the worst?

Shelly: Yes, because it affects the whole country. The Second World War continued for almost six years and we had to fight and suffer – all of us – to defeat the devil Adolf Hitler from conquering the whole world. We lived in

fear, but we had to fight. And we used
to say that we were all in the same boat.
That helped us not to give up.

Annie: Do you live in fear now?

Shelly: Not so much, now. I stay safely at
home most of the time, and when I'm
out, I'm with relatives – with you, for
example – and I feel safe most of the
time.

Annie: But you didn't like to take the
subway the other day!

Shelly: You're very observant, Annie! I
didn't feel well because I thought there
could be a bomb placed anywhere on
the line. But I'm glad we did it; next
time I'll feel better. And it's a long time
between the attacks compared with
the war.

Annie: Is terrorism a sort of war too?

Shelly: Good question, Annie! No, it isn't.
War is constant, but terrorist attacks are
rare and usually isolated. The similarity
is that the terrorists work to create fear,
and destroy our safe and good society,
and therefore we have to conquer our
fear, but that isn't easy. We must live like

before, and trust in the protection we receive from the police and government. And we must find ways to stop young people being recruited to terrorism.

Annie: How do you think we can do that?

Shelly: The only thing I believe in is that we need to make a better life and future for everyone, especially young boys without work and education, and to find those who teach them to kill in the name of their religion. They are criminals who mislead the boys. That's my opinion – you may say that if you talk about it in class tomorrow. From a very old lady.

Annie: A very wise old lady, I'd say!

Shelly: Thank you very much, my dear little wise Annie!

• • • • • • • • • • • • • •

What's new today?

In the old days, when a dreadful act happened in another country, we didn't hear about it for ages.

We certainly never saw it. But today, television and social media bring pictures of awful things into our homes almost immediately. We see the explosions; we see the dreadful wounds; we see people who are upset, and we get upset ourselves. Often, we start to worry that such a terrorist act could happen to us and we feel very afraid. As terrorists use more and more extreme ways to hurt people, the more the news on TV shows pictures of them and the more scared we can all become. Yes, we say 'we' because adults also feel scared, even though they try not to show it in front of children. But overall the world is a much more peaceful and safer place than it was hundreds of years ago, except maybe in the Middle East.

How can you better understand why terrorists do what they do?
How can they do these things?

How someone can kill innocent people in a terror attack is hard to understand. Adults have the same question as you kids do. When there are news reports about horrible and deadly terrorist attacks on innocent people, adults as well as children ask: Why did they do it? How can a young man shoot into a crowd, or drive a lorry at pedestrians, or blow himself to death to kill people in a crowd by detonating his hidden belt of explosives?

It's extremely hard to understand. So, first, let's explain a little about how the brain develops. Everyone's born with billions of brain cells. They start connecting to each other at high speed from the start of life, and most of the human brain is built in childhood and young adulthood. The brain gradually builds a library out of language, thoughts and experience. Everyone, including those who become terrorists, will develop and shape their brain gradually. A person's family, the environment they live in and all their experiences will be part of the building blocks that form their brain. One of the most important building blocks of the brain is good guidelines for how to act and behave among other people, in the family, at school and in society. One important part of these guidelines for behaviour is something called 'belief systems'. We all learn beliefs about how to behave towards other people from our parents, our family and friends, and from religion; we learn things like helping people in need, protecting them from sufferings, giving food or money to the poor, and so on.

As the brain develops, it also builds our centres for emotion. This area of the brain is called the 'emotional brain'. This is where people handle danger and learn to fight or flee if they're threatened. This is important for surviving dangerous situations. This part of the brain has no language, but it may have memories from bad experiences during childhood. It is thought that some terrorists have a huge network of bad memories from the past, so that their emotional brain is filled with unpleasant feelings that may cause angry, hostile and aggressive thoughts – thoughts that can make them seek ways to take revenge, even against innocent and unknown persons. Although it may not be possible to fully understand a terrorist's choice to do violent acts, many people believe that bad acts are more common after experiences of war and conflict. The emotional brain of terrorists may then be filled with very bad memories. If they've also lived in conditions of poverty and fear during their childhood, maybe with families who aren't able to care properly for them, they're more likely to become terrorists.

Terrorism has many names and many explanations

Terrorism has also been called *the language of the powerless, the desperate*. When people live in desperate need or poverty, they may blame others for their miserable situation. They may blame rich nations and rich people in power, with all the money and opportunities they have.

There are several reasons why people or groups use terrorism. All of these reasons are about wanting to achieve something. Most often, terrorists want to scare people, but they also want to provoke a reaction and to make a statement. Terrorists want to send a scary message to those in power or government, and they know that if they attack innocent people, they get more attention than if they attack just buildings or the military. If they think that a few people earn a lot of money in a poor country and keep it for themselves, a terror attack at a popular site may scare away tourists. Then, or so they believe, the selfish rich people in the country lose money.

In many of the countries with terrorist groups, people live in poverty, and many countries have experienced wars and unrest. Many people believe that much of the turmoil that's going on in the world is because of bad leaders who've become wealthy themselves, while the rest of the people live in poverty and distress and have no work. The terrorists blame this on other nations, particularly the USA and Europe. It may be true that these countries have a past history of suppressing other countries and stealing their resources. You may have learned about this in history lessons. Many European countries have a history of what's called 'exploiting' others (becoming rich by using what belongs to others).

Most often in terrorism, the terrorists want other people to think like them. They won't accept or believe that this can be done peacefully or differently. Some want to draw attention to their situation so that others become aware of how they feel. Their situation may be terrible, but most people condemn their choice to let terror affect innocent people. There are also 'lone terrorists' who aren't working with other people or in a group, but they may feel that they've been wronged all their life. Some may have had a childhood where they were bullied and they want revenge for that, or they may have psychiatric problems. This is explained in more detail in the next section, which talks about how their brakes and cleaning machine don't function properly.

Mass killings in rich countries aren't usually committed by people called terrorists. The reasons why these people who aren't terrorists act in this way vary. Some have lost their jobs days before, others have been bullied or isolated at work or school, and some have had serious mental health problems without getting proper help. Most of these killers have had very few friends. Many psychologists therefore believe that their brains must have been filled with chaotic thoughts and that their actions express desperation and feelings of hopelessness.

Young people who don't feel part of society, who feel left out and have few friends, may be more likely to join terrorist groups or commit mass killings. In a terrorist group they may feel more valued. Being part of a group where they feel welcome and accepted may be very important for them, regardless of the group's ideas and actions. If this way of understanding why people become terrorists is correct, it means that one way to reduce terrorism is to look at why young people feel isolated or left out of society. By working for a society where young people feel included and worthy, terrorism can be reduced.

Brakes and cleaning machine

So far, we've explained some of the reasons why someone may become a terrorist that are to do with society. But what happens inside a person's mind? We'll introduce some words to help you understand this. These words are called 'concepts' and they help us to understand how terrorists think. This is what we authors, as psychologists, do; we try to understand feelings and thoughts.

All people have a *brake* in their mind that they can step on for stopping dangerous thoughts, and they have a *cleaning machine* that quickly removes the worst thoughts. Everyone does and says stupid things sometimes. It's completely normal. Afterwards, most people apologise. The brake and the cleaning machine are most people's familiar, good friends.

With the help of parents and friends, the vast majority of people gradually learn when to apply brakes or 'clean up' thoughts that go astray. Unfortunately, in a few people the brake and the cleaning machine function poorly, maybe because the person experienced many terrible things in childhood. It can be for other reasons too. It's also possible that the brain gets poisoned and full of crazy and angry thoughts because of the people terrorists keep company with. The main thing we want you to understand is that it's very rare for anyone to get such bad thoughts that it makes them kill innocent people.

At present in Europe, a lot of the time we hear most about terrorist acts linked to countries that are Muslim. But terrorists can be found in many countries. Most people around the world, whether they're in Muslim countries or other countries, don't want war or terrorism. They're ordinary people who want to live in peace. But there are some groups in different countries who have guns and bombs. They're criminals because they kill or threaten to kill innocent people. They use terror to scare people. Some individuals may have got the idea of harming others from what they've seen in the media and then copied that in their own terror attack. When something gets a lot of attention in the media, it increases the risk of other people copying the behaviour.

People commit terrorist acts for different reasons. We believe that people need better ways to discover when young people's brains are becoming filled with ideas and hate that can end in terror acts. People need to work to better understand the power of religion and belief systems. But at the same time people also need to notice when young people feel very alone, when they feel excluded from the rest of society, or end up feeling valued only in groups that accept ideas that include the killing of innocent people. Many people firmly believe that good and deep friendships and the love of others, including across cultural differences, may prevent someone from ending up as a terrorist. Helping people to feel included and valued in life, even when they're different from us, is a responsibility shared by children and adults alike. This is why cultural understanding is such a big part of what you learn at school.

The risk of being involved in a terrorist attack

Watching reports of terrorist attacks from many different countries, it sometimes feels that every day you might be hurt in one. But when was the last time you saw a terrorist attack in real life? The reality is that they're very rare. You need to remember that your brain plays tricks on you.

Everyone's does. When you hear about a plane crashing and see pictures on TV, you might think it's very dangerous to fly. But it isn't. When you think of the thousands of planes that take off and land every day in hundreds of airports all over the world, you can see that plane crashes are extremely rare. The same is true of terrorist attacks. All the attention they get makes everyone think they happen much more often than they do.

The risk that you'll be where a terror attack happens is very low. But what is a low risk? We'll use an example to illustrate this. If something happens almost every day – for example, your teacher saying 'good morning' to you – you could say the risk of hearing your teacher say 'good morning' is high. If you think of something that happens quite often, such as a change in weather, you'd say the risk of the weather changing is moderate. If it was something that only happened very rarely, such as the teacher saying you can take the rest of the day off, you'd say that the risk of this happening is very low. Well, the risk of a terrorist attack happening to you is very, very, very low. This doesn't mean it can't happen, but it happens so rarely that there's no need to go around thinking about it.

The problem is that sometimes your feelings take charge and decide that you're going to be afraid. Your rational thoughts about what the risk is are overruled by your feelings. And as you've learned, media attention can play tricks on our feelings – anyone can become afraid and think that what they saw will happen to them. Even adults who know that the risk is very low can be concerned, worried and sometimes afraid. If you become afraid, that's when you must fight the anxious thoughts by telling yourself that you're safe. More about that later.

This is how low the risk is: you could probably travel from one capital city in Europe like London, Paris, Berlin, Vienna, Stockholm and Brussels to another, day in and day out for many years, and still never witness a terror attack. But although you tell yourself that it's best not to think about such an attack, sometimes you're worried and afraid, and that's OK. If that's the case, then you can do the things we write about later, such as telling an adult or thinking about something else.

I'm afraid of terrorists

A conversation between a father and his nine-year-old son, Tony

Tony: Dad, I'm afraid of terrorists!

Father: You are? Tell me about when you feel like this, Tony.

Tony: For days after I've seen something about terrorism on TV, I look everywhere when I'm walking outside, even on the safe route to school. Last Sunday on the subway I almost panicked when I saw those strange people carrying strange bags.

Father: It's good that you're telling me this. I can tell you that the chance of you being hit by a terrorist attack is incredibly small.

Tony: But it's happened everywhere! Almost everywhere in Europe, America, and many other places.

Father: If you think of the 500 million people living in Europe, and you count the victims of terror, the numbers will almost be microscopic. And so are the chances of you and me being hit, son!

Tony: But we're told to be observant when strange things happen!

Father: I know that, but personally, I don't think it's good advice to give to children. There are so many things and events happening outside that may look strange that you may end up being afraid of everything, everywhere. Of course, if you find yourself in the middle of something dangerous, frightening or scary, you can tell an adult or find somewhere to hide.

Tony: Wouldn't you be afraid if a bomb exploded in the supermarket down the road tomorrow?

Father: I'd feel very sorry for those who were hurt, I'd want them to get the best help to survive, and I'd want the police to hunt for the terrorist, but the next day I'd go to the nearest supermarket and buy my stuff, without being afraid. I don't want fear or terrorists to ruin my daily life.

Tony: You're very brave, Dad!

Father: Well, I'm not that brave, but I've lived much longer than you, and it isn't so easy to make me panic. I'm worried, but not really frightened, because I think that the enormous attention that TV and media give terrorism gives us a false feeling that it happens everywhere all the time. That's not the case.

Tony: It was good to talk to you, Dad!

Father: I think we should talk more often.

· · · · · · · · · · · · · ·

What can be done to reduce the risk of a terrorist attack?

You already know how to reduce the risk of getting harmed by rare events. Even though the risk is low, it's sensible to think how you can reduce it even further. So – what did you learn about crossing roads? It's sensible to stop, look left and right and listen before crossing a road, and even better to use a crossing place if there's one nearby. When you go out on a boat, even though you think you're a good swimmer, you wear a life jacket

– just in case there's an accident, even though there's only a very small risk of one happening. Then you'll survive. When the fire alarm rings in school, you've already practised walking safely out of the building. All these are low-risk events, but you reduce the risk even further by practising what to do. That's much better than worrying about them the whole time.

How do our national governments and institutions act to prevent terror?

In European countries, and other so-called Western countries like the USA, Canada, New Zealand and Australia, we rely on the police.

They have systems for monitoring the phones and internet activity of those suspected of planning terrorism. They can stop terrorists before they do something. They've done this before, and they'll do so again. If they learn that there's a danger or threat of terrorism, they'll take precautions to prevent something from happening. They'll monitor and protect airports, trains, buses and important buildings where the government is located. Where large numbers of people gather, such as at events in the centre of towns and cities, at museums or pop concerts, they'll also be more alert. Nevertheless, we can never say that terrorism can't happen. We can't control everything.

What is being done to address the causes?

For the next decades the 194 member countries of the United Nations (UN) have formulated several global goals, and at least three of these are very relevant to the prevention of terrorism.

The number one goal is to remove poverty. This is a good goal for many reasons. We know that situations of unrest, planning for war, attacking governments and so on may happen more readily in very poor countries or societies. Therefore this global goal will also help prevent terrorist acts.

The UN also proposes that all their member states should work to reduce inequalities between groups of people in their country. This can reduce sources of anger and aggression among the poorest groups in the population.

Both of these goals address poor living conditions for children and their families. These conditions may create a climate for recruiting young people to commit terrorist acts. We know that the millions of refugees around the world can live under especially poor conditions, and they may not be able to imagine any future where normal life resumes. Without any hope for the future, people have little to lose and may more easily become terrorists.

The third goal that will help to reduce terrorism is the UN global goal to work for peace and justice in all member states. We know that both war and injustice may cause unrest and crime and encourage terrorism. By attaching high importance to this, the UN is working to reduce terrorism.

The Convention on the Rights of the Child

For more than a hundred years we've known how growing up in very difficult life conditions is damaging to a person. Around 1890 a movement was formed in Liverpool, in the UK, called the Liverpool Society for the Prevention of Cruelty against Children, and soon it became a national society and a movement that spread throughout Europe. Cruelty in childhood created too many sick, violent and criminal members of society. It had to be prevented, and several child protection laws were established. A hundred years later, in 1989, the Convention on the Rights of the Child (CRC) was agreed on to protect children, and it's signed by 193 of the UN's 194 member states (only the USA hasn't adopted it). The CRC, the world's international law for children, gives children freedom of speech similar to that of adults (Article 13). The CRC states that children should be encouraged and trained in claiming the rights that are given to them in this declaration. Adults should, together with children, demand better protection with reference to the CRC. Article 17 of the CRC promises that the media should consider children and give them access to accurate information and protect them from harmful reports. A natural consequence of Article 17 would be to have appropriate national news for children.

Article 39 gives children rights to psychological recovery and social rehabilitation after exposure to *inhuman, degrading treatment.* Children are granted help to regain normal lives after a terrorist attack.

Article 19 demands that the UN member states should prevent physical and psychological violence against children, and bad living conditions for children and young people. These are conditions that may create a climate for recruiting young people to commit terrorist acts. This is directly connected to Article 2, one of the four strongest articles in the CRC: the prohibition of any discrimination. It's relevant to fighting terrorism since ghettos of poor children and young people who are discriminated against as refugees may also promote recruitment to terrorist organisations – young people can believe they've no future and therefore feel they've nothing to lose. This is reinforced in Article 39 which says that child victims of violent attacks and experiences should be helped to regain normality.

Articles 28 and 29 are about children's rights to education. They emphasise that children should be taught and brought up to live responsible lives in free societies that promote friendship with people of all nationalities, religions and ethnic origins. This article is also relevant to prevent conditions that can lead to terrorism.

What can the media do?

We've talked about how terrorists and other mass killers want to create fear or get attention through their acts. We think that terrorism and mass killings could be reduced if the media became more careful and less sensational in what they present. We also want them to help people understand more about why terrorists commit such acts, instead of showing many horrible pictures of dead and badly injured people. The media could make sensible choices about what to report and what not to report. Experts are clear: reduced media coverage will result in fewer terrorist and mass killings. We believe that a good step forward would be to restrict media coverage that gives attention to terrorists and mass killers.

A statement about those who carry out mass shootings, signed by 149 experts, has criticised the media for the sensational way it covers terrorism, school shootings and other mass killings.[1] Terrorists and other killers seek attention and media coverage; they may even claim responsibility for acts that they didn't commit, to get the attention they require and achieve their main aim: producing fear! The experts claim that the media gives the killers exactly what they ask for: giving them attention and causing fear. The killers know they'll be famous even after their own

---

1   Lankford, A. and Madfis, E. (2018) 'Media coverage of mass killers: content, consequences, and solutions.' *American Behavioral Scientist 62*, 2, 151–162.

death. The experts also fear that the attention given to terrorist attacks will be a motive for others to do the same.

What do nations and communities do to help when societies are hit and people are killed by terrorists?

Doctors, nurses and emergency responders – the police, ambulance and fire services – act quickly to help and save as many lives as they can. Some victims must be treated at hospitals; others need less help.

Because those who come close to such events can experience difficult feelings and thoughts afterwards, there are other helpers such as us – psychologists – who assist those who need help to get back to leading more normal lives again. Many need information about how it's normal to react. Most people will gradually resume their usual life. Those who lose someone they love can continue to experience much pain and grief over a long time and will often benefit from help from family, friends and health workers.

Following a terrorist attack in a particular country, national leaders such as the royal family, the president, the prime minister or the mayor offer their support. It's important that those who are affected by such events feel that they have many people who support them.

People are strong together, and often those who are directly affected by terror attacks form their own support groups where they can meet and feel togetherness. Few know exactly what it's like to be affected by terror as well as other survivors and bereaved do, and together they can support and help each other. There are also bonds formed between those who experienced previous terror attacks and those who experience new events.

It's very good that people can comfort and help each other and reduce feelings of being alone in their situation.

What can you do if you become worried or afraid?

Live normally

It isn't possible to know where or when a terrorist attack will take place. It also happens very rarely. This means that it's useless to spend too much time thinking about terrorism. Thinking about it doesn't prevent it, nor does it help us. You might think that it would help if you made a plan of what to do, but what to plan for is difficult or impossible to know. If you start thinking about it, it makes you worried and you waste energy on this. Worry interferes with your concentration and memory. We think that the best thing to do is to live life in a normal way. Go to school, take part in sports activities, and have fun. If you let yourself be intimidated, the terrorists 'win', because they aim to make all of us so scared that we can't live as we want. The terrorists always want everyone to be afraid. But we're safe and have nothing to fear. There are very few terrorists, and they can't be in many places at once.

Try not to worry

Some children worry a lot. If you're among them, here is a tip for worrying less. Set aside a time for worrying each day (or every other day if you worry a little less) but not more than 15 minutes. This is your worry time. Here you can address your worries, list them, and look at them from different angles. You can think about the risk and list the reasons that you think your worry will become a fact on one side – and then on the other side, list things that make it less likely your worries will come true. If your worries bubble up (and they usually will if you worry a lot), just notice this, and don't get annoyed or irritated. Just say to yourself: 'I'm not going to think about this now but in my worry time.' Do this every time the worry comes up – be patient with yourself. Gradually, the worry thoughts will stop automatically. But you must practise. This way of postponing a worry has helped many children with worries.

Distract yourself

If the risk of terror is so low, it'll only be stressful to think of this. Doing other things, being active with sports, being with friends and similar activities help you take your thoughts away and at the same time defeats the terrorists. Why? Because you won't feel frightened, which is what they want you to feel.

If you worry a lot, make a plan

This concept is a bit strange. We've already said you can't know when or where a terrorist attack might happen, as it happens so very rarely. That makes it very difficult to make concrete plans for such a situation. But if you worry a lot, it might be good to have gone through in your mind some of the things you can do. 'If I hear shooting, I'll seek cover and hide'; 'If I see a car that runs wild, I'll look for where to escape and hide behind a solid object'. A simple plan can be to remember in your mind how to call up emergency services by phone, or to contact a person in uniform. These are action plans or things that you can repeat in your mind a few times. They can ease your worry. If you've thought through what you can do if such and such an event happens, you can call up these plans when you start to worry. Just remind yourself that you have a plan of what to do, to ease your worry.

Think strong thoughts

You can steer your thoughts and calm your worries by what you say to yourself. You can talk to yourself, telling your mind things that calm you down and make you feel safe. Such thoughts are:

> 'The police watch out for us.'

> 'I'm safe.'

> 'I can calm my thoughts.'

> 'There's very little chance of a terrorist attack happening to me.'

Try to find your own strong thoughts and make a list of them.

Remember, it helps to share your thoughts and worries, and it helps to talk about them.

Do adults get afraid?

Of course they do – sometimes. But after a terrorist attack they say things like 'We're not afraid', 'Back to normal tomorrow', 'Take back the streets' and 'They'll never scare us, we have no fear'. They say these things to convince themselves, to try to show children not to be afraid either, and to tell the terrorists they haven't succeeded in scaring people. If such attacks didn't make adults afraid, why would they be given so much importance in the media? It can be confusing when you sense that adults are afraid but hear them say they aren't. We know that adults can be frightened. But more than frightened, they become horrified by terror and the news in the media. Such reactions are normal and human. You may react the same way when you hear about it. Everyone cares about what happens to other people.

If you hear politicians and others say that 'We're not afraid', that's because this boosts morale and make us feel stronger together. But adults get worried and you may sense that, or they may tell you directly. Like you, adults can be afraid that it'll happen to them. Parents become especially worried that something will happen to their children – to you. Some adults might change their holiday or travel plans, and you know that they're worried when they do this.

Sometimes when they say 'Don't worry' or say that they don't worry themselves, they're hiding their own worry. When terrorist acts get so much attention in the media, adults too will think that attacks happen more frequently than they actually do. So, think back to what we've already said: very few people die from terror attacks each year – you just think it's more dangerous than it is because of the news. We can't say that terror isn't dangerous. It can be deadly. But there's very little chance of us being a victim of a terrorist attack.

Part 2

• • • • •

How to Explain
Terrorism to Children

TERROR AND CHILDREN

Throughout childhood, children are developing their sense of security in their world. Their concepts or assumptions about the world, about others and themselves, are formed in the interaction with you, the significant adults in their lives – whether you're their teachers, their parents or professionals working with them – as well as with their friends and their community. In addition, the media and modern forms of communication affect their development and how they view risks in their close and more distant environment. Terror becomes part of their lifeworld as it gets much media attention.

When a terrorist act is reported in the news, a child will learn of it and will quite likely ask you questions. This is the time to answer their questions. First, ask them what they've heard; what they understand about 'terrorism'. You need to answer them honestly, but not necessarily give them all the gory details. You need to admit that you're concerned but also to reassure them as far as possible. Here we give more suggestions on how to do this. It's intended to help all adults with responsibility for children, as teachers, parents and grandparents, or in other non-professional or professional roles.

WHY IS IT IMPORTANT TO TALK TO CHILDREN?

The coverage from terror attacks contains very graphic pictures and situations. The images are played over and over, and the news reaches children through the front pages of newspapers, and on TV, the radio and internet. Seeing dead and mutilated bodies, people in fear for their life and physical destruction affects children's minds. Many children follow the news and update themselves on what's happening when terror strikes, and yet they struggle to understand what has happened. According to nurseries and kindergartens, as well as parents, children as young as four and five are concerned about what they've seen on TV. Children may talk among themselves about this and then continue to think about it afterwards.

So you can almost take it for granted that a child has probably heard or read more about terrorism than you think. News travels fast in children's worlds. If they haven't heard about it directly from the media, then friends and schoolmates have. Repeatedly, we've learned of children knowing about serious events to a much greater extent than their parents or teachers have thought. If you leave them to process such events alone, they'll deal with upsetting news mixed with misconceptions and everyone's emotional reactions, while their life experience puts limits on their ability to process what they take in on their own. For this reason, we advocate a proactive approach from teachers, parents and other adults looking after children. Address the issue, explain and discuss, be open for questions, and help them understand.

It's important to highlight that many children, even though they're both frightened and upset, don't necessarily find that violent news interferes with their daily lives. If a child is behaving just as before, it's important that you don't pressure them into a daily conversations where they must deal with issues of terrorism. But you must have your 'antennae' on relatively high alert, because there are many children who can seem totally unconcerned, but this is only because they don't want to bother their parents or teachers.

There's no shortage of reports on anxious children who don't speak with their mum and dad or their teacher. To our question about why, they have a standard response which we believe to be true: 'Adults don't know how to answer.'

THE NEED TO UNDERSTAND – PROVIDING PEGS

When you explain dramatic news to children, especially following terror events, there are two approaches you need to use and keep in mind.

The first and most important is called the 'therapeutic' approach. When you explain, curb unnecessary agitation and anxiety regarding what can happen to the child or young person themselves. As a rule, it's not enough to say that grown-ups aren't afraid, although it's important to be a calm role model. Part of this therapeutic approach is to accept that a child may naturally seek more adult proximity, such as being clingier or seeking more attention at bedtime.

The other approach is called 'educational'. News about terror upsets adults and children, but although it's terrible news, it can give rise to important learning. It provides parents and teachers with an opportunity to educate their child about the world, other people, and even politics and religion, as well as teaching them how to regulate emotions and bodily reactions. You need to help them establish pegs that enhance their understanding and emotional regulation strategies that they can use throughout life. This educational approach also relates to the therapeutic approach as it helps the child to get a cognitive grip on what has happened and to comprehend how someone could do this.

It's hard to fathom that anyone can do something so terrible as to carry out a terrorist attack. Adults have pegs that they put their anxieties on that prevent them from continuously thinking that a terrorist attack could happen at any time in their neighbourhood. It's this adult confidence that children should develop. It's therefore important to explain to children that such terrorist acts are very, very rare. It doesn't make the acts less terrible, but it'll allow children to be protected from constantly thinking that it can happen here and now, any time. Good information dampens children's anxiety. It's hard to explain that something is rare to a very young child, but when they're closer to school age, they understand that Christmas, Eid or Pesach come only once a year, as does their birthday. When you explain frequency and chance in comparison to events they know, they can get an understanding of why they shouldn't think that it can happen any time. See how we explain this risk in the section 'The risk of being involved in a terrorist attack' in Part 1.

HOW TO BREAK THE NEWS

Some terror events immediately cover all news channels. If that's the case, we advise that you get on top of the situation by informing your children as early as possible. How can you do this? Here is a suggested opening with an example of a lorry being driven into a crowd:

> I just learned that there has been a terror event in X. There are many people dead and injured. We know of no one in our family that was in X when this happened. What we know happened was that a truck was driven into a large crowd of people before it could be stopped. It was stopped, but not until many people had been injured and killed. They're doing everything they can to help those who were

injured. I wanted to tell you this before you heard about it from friends or saw it on the internet or television. When we know more about this, I'll tell you what's new if you want me to. I don't think it's a good idea for you to watch much about this on the news – that can make you upset and start you worrying. Because such terror events get so much attention, we think they happen more frequently than they really do. In fact, it's very rare that such events happen. If there's anything you want to ask me or talk about, I'm here for you.

Give them the relevant facts and basic information about what happened. There's no need to overload them with details, and no need for them to see horrific pictures of mutilated or bloodied bodies or injured people. Emphasise that there are plans in place to help people when something like this happens, not only with their injuries but also to comfort and assist them if they feel upset or worried afterwards.

THE NEED TO BE COMFORTING AND CALMING

Children become worried by terror attacks and they may think that this can happen to their loved ones and themselves. They need adult comfort and understanding. What we've written about helping them to understand also comforts them. Good information almost always helps children and adults alike to calm down; it dampens our fantasies and eases our worries. A calm adult presence, where the children's thoughts are being met by information and conversations where they can elaborate and get perspective on their own thinking, helps them get a better grip of what terrorism is and how unlikely they are to experience it personally.

A major component of this book is about how you can reassure children. You can do this in the following ways:

1. Explain how the risk of terror can be overestimated. Try to explain how this results from media attention and the mental mechanism of mistaking the sensationalised for the frequent.

2. Explain the different ways that the UN, the government and the police do all they can to reduce terrorism.

3. 'Teach' or inform children about what they can do to control their worries. They learn to take control of their thoughts by a specific worry method, and by using distraction and strong thoughts.

The methods taught to children can also be used by adults themselves to regulate their worries, and we suggest that you guide your children in this. You may know of other ways that have worked well with your children in the past that can supplement what we've written.

CALM BEHAVIOUR FROM GROWN-UPS PRODUCES CALM CHILDREN

As a teacher, parent or carer, you play the major role in calming the child or children in your care. You do this first and foremost through your behaviour. You remain calm, and by this you 'infect' the child with your calmness. This refers not only to your behaviour when you watch news and children are present, but even more so when you sit down to explain terrorism to them. A calm, direct and honest approach will have a soothing effect on them. It'll bring their cognitions online and help them to think about what you're telling them or discussing with them, instead of making them more emotional. You'll also be a good role model for them. We have many reports telling us that children simply don't remember what they're told if they, their parents or both are upset during the conversation. It's also good to check that the child can repeat the message back properly. Do this carefully so they don't feel that they're taking a test!

It's all right for them to continue with everyday activities. Keeping up ordinary routines is in fact very useful to signal and establish normality and structure when horrible events take place. It provides a sense of security to both children and adults.

APPROACHING CONVERSATIONS
Being open and honest

As three psychologists working with grief and trauma, we have ourselves over our lifetimes been faced with very difficult situations regarding what to say when a parent has committed suicide or been diagnosed with cancer, or situations where individuals or groups of children have been sexually abused. The question of what, how much and when to tell children is always an issue.

The lesson we've learned, regardless of the situation, is that it's best to be open, honest and direct. As soon as you underestimate children's need to know and to understand, or you think that something's too painful to inform them about, you're entering a cobweb of concealment and secrets that at some point backfires.

We therefore advise you to be open and honest. Sometimes you'll need a little time to answer a difficult question, but don't let your wish to protect your child get the better of you. Things can be hard for them to hear about, but a child's trust in you will always increase if you're honest and straightforward with them.

Also remember that children learn about such events from sources other than you anyway. If you hold back information or present an edited story, they may see through this and lose trust in the information you give them. They may also pick up on the cue that you aren't comfortable talking about this and subsequently avoid discussing the subject with you. If you don't bring up the subject at all and the child is upset or worried about what has happened, they may think that you're uninterested or unwilling to discuss it.

Starting a conversation

After a terrorist attack has occurred, you can be very matter-of-fact when starting a conversation with your child (see the example in the section 'How to break the news' above). If a terror attack has happened before you see the child, just ask them if they've heard about what happened and take it from there. Ask them what they've heard and what their friends and schoolmates say about this. This can reveal misunderstandings and give you a feel for how the child or children have reacted to the event. Immediately after a terror attack, there's usually a lack of information and lots of rumours. If you have additional information, you may fill in gaps in their understanding. You can also correct misunderstandings. This may not be the time to have a lengthy conversation, but you can convey the message that you're there if they want to talk, and that you'll return to the subject later.

If you're a parent and the event occurs while you're at home, be proactive and tell the child what has happened, but don't keep the television news on all the time. Explain why it's better to get a few updates than to watch such news continually. You shouldn't ban children from watching *some* news reports, but evidence shows that the more children watch accounts of the same atrocity, the more likely they are to get upset. As always, it can be difficult to strike the right balance between being open and being too protective.

Timing is also important. It isn't a good idea to start a conversation close to bedtime. A better time is after school, before dinner. Remember that many children talk most when there's some other activity going on – for example, when you're driving in the car or walking to an activity. Long conversations about serious issues aren't usually what children have in mind; they often push adults out, only to restart the conversation later. If you see a child hesitating to participate in an activity that's usually enjoyable for them – such as going to a concert, a shopping centre or a sports game – we'd suggest that you ask them if there's anything they're worried about, and then take the conversation from there.

If they ask questions, answer as truthfully as you can. If you don't know the answer, say that you'll find out and come back to them. We sometimes refer to elaborative conversations, which means helping children to expand their understanding by following their line of thinking and expanding on it. Have them explain what they mean and touch their thoughts with adult reasoning. Let them set the pace, but be willing to lead a conversation. Listen to what's behind their questions (i.e. worry and concern) and be less concerned about voicing your own views. If your attempt at conversation is met by resistance, try again later. Sometimes a little persistence is needed before children open up.

When you've explained something, a good tip is to ask your child to tell it back to you. They won't use the exact words you did, but any misunderstanding will quickly be obvious, and you may have to find simpler ways of explaining.

USING YOUR ANTENNAE

If you're a parent, then you know your child better than anyone. If you're a teacher, you're a person who spends a great deal of time with the children in your class. Adults coming into contact with children can often read signs of discomfort or worry. Following terror events, you may pick up signals – from their questions, by overhearing bits of conversations they have with friends, or if they seem more interested in the news than usual – that show that they're concerned about what has happened. Similarly, you may pick up signs from their behaviour – such as problems falling or staying asleep, nightmares, issues with their friends at playtime or problems concentrating in class – that are different from usual. In other words, by being sensitive to signals from the child and changes in their behaviour, you can see that you need to start a conversation or hear if they're worried. A last reminder here is related to the fact that children often don't differentiate between being upset and being scared. Adults may be upset because of gruesome acts, but the acts may not necessarily scare them in their daily lives. You can help children to understand the difference.

FINDING WAYS OF EXPLAINING

Although there have been terror attacks in several countries and cities over the last few years, you should explain to the child that very few people die from terrorism compared with illness or accidents. If they're above ten years of age, you can also tell them that within a few months many more people in Europe die from taking their own life than are killed in terror attacks. This isn't to make them more afraid of these kinds of deaths, but to explain that whenever there's a terror attack or a disaster, the media depicts it in such graphic detail in the news that we as humans become more afraid that something like that will happen again. Society tends to fear the spectacular more than much more common causes of death. If you find it appropriate with your child, you may compare the number of terror victims with figures from car accidents.

When terrorist acts happen, or other terrible news dominates the media, we recommend that you actively observe your children and how preoccupied they are by this. It's better for you to start up a conversation with them than to think that they probably haven't registered what has happened. Responsible adults don't leave children to their own thoughts and imaginings, but ensure that the conversation can meet any fears they have and answer their questions. We think it's correct to convey to your children that as an adult you've noted that the police have learned a lot from previous horrific events and that therefore they've become better able to protect everyone and both you and your children can feel safer than before.

WHAT CAN YOU SAY ABOUT TERROR, TERRORISM AND TERRORISTS?

The words 'terror', 'terrorism' and 'terrorists' are used differently from country to country. In Part 1, you can read about how you can explain these concepts for children. We've tried to reserve the concept of terrorism to what goes on outside of war, for those who kill innocent people who don't have weapons. We haven't explained state terrorism for children in order not to make it too complex. If you have adolescent children, they may ask you questions about this and you'll need to read up on such aspects to answer them well. You can even search the internet together and look at and discuss what you find there. We've written about different causes of terrorism to help them understand that the concept of terrorism isn't straightforward to explain, and that terrorism can have many roots (see the section 'Terrorism has many names and many explanations' in Part 1).

This also means that you may not agree with the way we've presented it and want to bring in your own views. That's OK, of course, but we ask you to try to explain in a neutral tone if possible. Presenting this material or discussing it with too much emotion will easily cloud the issues and make it more difficult to reason and understand. For example, if Islam is depicted in a very derogatory, negative way, that can easily transfer into opinions and behaviour that later can be expressed in negative behaviour towards all Muslims, including classmates, neighbours or other people the children meet. You are, of course, a role model in all your behaviour.

We've chosen to talk about the aim of terror being to frighten. We've made use of simple descriptions of mental mechanisms, such as 'brakes' and 'cleaning machine' (see next section). Obviously, what makes terrorists do what they do may reflect more complex mechanisms. Terrorism results from complex processes, at the individual, group and societal level. However, the empathy that stops most people from hurting others isn't functioning in those who become terrorists. This means that individuals responsible for terror have suspended their necessary stop mechanisms. We believe that, in explaining this to children, you need concepts that are easy for them to understand. We do acknowledge that the function of the ideology of the group to which the terrorist belongs partly explains why terror breeds.

We've introduced different factors, both individual (bad memories) and environmental (poverty, oppression), in our explanations. Children try to make sense of their world. As an adult, you must strike a balance between simple, understandable explanations and the more complex reality that's hard to understand for most people. There are many ways of explaining why terrorism is carried out by groups from different religions. You can't refrain from a brief explanation of why you think this is so, at the same time emphasising that only a few followers take part in this.

ABOUT WRONG THOUGHTS AND THE MIND'S CLEANING MACHINE

We've struggled to find concepts that can be used to explain how terrorists are thinking. This isn't easy, as every explanation can reflect a political view. We do, however, think it's right to explain that individuals who plan to kill innocent people – by shooting them, bringing down a plane, driving a truck into crowds of people – have wrong thoughts in their mind, bordering on a disease in their mind – what we sometimes call *thinking diseases*, to simplify it for children.

We also believe that it's important to address some of the roots of terrorism, not only explaining this as a result of individual thoughts gone wrong. In Part 1 we explained how the living conditions of those who become terrorists and their experiences during childhood, including war, can be part of what causes terrorism. We tried to convey that we don't have all the answers and that terrorism may have many and different causes. We strongly believe that adults must meet children's need to understand. This means that their thoughts and cognitions are met with discussions and explanations. Their worries increase with a lack of understanding.

Two concepts that you can use are 'brakes' and 'cleaning machine'. The fact that someone first plans to kill and then actually does kill innocent people can be illustrated by explaining to the children that all people can have strange and sometimes dangerous thoughts, but in their mind they have brakes that hinder them from acting upon the thoughts. The children know they can get into trouble if they hit someone in class, so they put on their brakes. The brain has a tidying or cleaning machine that constantly watches out for wrong thoughts, and it'll start the brakes when necessary. In terrorists, however, the brakes aren't applied; there's nothing to stop the wrong thoughts. The brakes aren't used, and the cleaning machine is broken. In internet groups, terrorists have little contact with people other than those with similar ideas, and they can develop bad ideas and thoughts together and agree to act on those wrong thoughts. Most of what we have written here applies to school shooters as well.

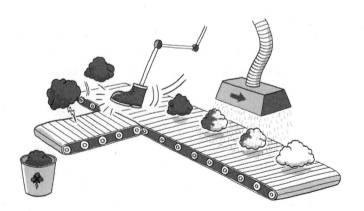

AGE-APPROPRIATE CONVERSATIONS

Conversations with children must be appropriate to their age and understanding. Adults often underestimate what children can understand because children ask us questions that reflect how little they know. Without facts and experience, their understanding will be limited. Left to themselves or to conversations with their peers, they're prone to misunderstandings, rumours, fears and fantasies. Therefore, when children feel strongly about what has happened, parents and teachers must meet children's need for understanding as well as for comfort and support.

Age 3–6 years

What the smallest children primarily need to hear is that they and you are safe. The youngest children are both protected and more vulnerable because of their limited language comprehension. They're partly protected because they think that mum and dad arrange everything, and everything is safe. The dangerous outside world has yet to enter their world. Nevertheless, they're also vulnerable in their lack of understanding of the way adults protect themselves and their families when they come to be in a place where there's terror. Although they're far away from where a terrorist attack happened, their understanding of distance is limited, and they can fear that it'll happen close to them. They may struggle to understand what happens, and they observe and take their cues about their own safety and what to do from their carers. If parents keep calm, reassure them of their safety and provide information for them to understand parents' reactions, they may cope well. It's difficult for children if they perceive a situation as dangerous and they have to put together the pieces on their own.

Age 7–12 years

Younger school-age children understand more and they increasingly become users of different media. This means that their exposure to what goes on in the world increases. Although they can seek out information on their own, this doesn't necessarily mean that they have the experience to understand and process this.

Children of this age engage more actively in such news because they understand more. They have distinct concepts about what a country is and know where certain cities are located on the globe, and they understand far more about the impact of terror acts. They also have concepts to understand that people can plan to kill others, they can be concerned for their own security, and they have political opinions regarding cause and effect. A last reminder here: children as young as eight years of age may seemingly understand everything, but they may lack a deeper understanding because of their limited life experience.

Age 13–18 years

Adolescents access different news media; they discuss a lot among themselves, and emotions can rapidly spread in a group. Although their understanding of events is more advanced than in younger children, their ability to think ahead about the ramifications of events is still limited. Their understanding and beliefs are increasingly influenced by friends. Emotions run high at this stage and fuel rumours, and exaggerations of what has happened can flourish. They can be very political and argumentative and, with emotions sometimes running high, it may not be easy to inform them about or discuss terror events.

KEEP TABS ON THEIR MEDIA INTAKE

One of the consistent research findings from recent years is the documentation of how much terror news negatively affects children (and adults). Children are becoming high consumers of news through different channels, even before they start school. Findings from research show that the more terror news they take in, the more afraid they are. Even children not directly affected by terror can develop post-traumatic symptoms such as getting intrusive memories from what they've seen on the news. Researchers have even used the term *second-hand terrorism* to refer to the omnipresent threat and insecurity that lingers in children's environment long after the terror (Comer and Kendall 2007). It's still unknown to what extent this influences a child, but as parents, teachers or carers you're needed as guides to help children understand and process what they take in through different media and internet sources. Remember also that social media rapidly spreads both true and untrue information and rumours.

This also means that as a parent, in particular, you need to keep track of your children's time on the internet or in front of the TV. We suggest that you try to watch the news after they have gone to bed. It's hard to keep kids off the internet, but by talking about how news affects them and employing slightly stricter 'surveillance' than usual, you can put restrictions on the amount of exposure they have to potentially upsetting news. You can also help them understand how news about terror attacks makes them believe disproportionately that terror attacks are very common and likely to happen to them. They may need to be more media literate to understand how the media relies on dramatic coverage to capture audiences and sell their product.

ADMITTING YOUR OWN WORRIES

Many adults are shocked about what takes place, and when familiar tourist sites are targeted, their feeling of safety is threatened. They react with sadness, anger, fear and worry. Children see how adults react and they sense the importance of such events from the way that the media is filled with coverage. Media slogans such as 'We aren't afraid', 'Back to normal tomorrow', 'Take back the 'streets' and 'They'll never scare us, we have no fear' are heard with great frequency. This adult rhetoric around how to cope and deal with the terror threat and our own fear, is reiterated by our political leaders in Churchill-like speeches, even in phrases like 'we shall never surrender'.

As psychologists, we of course see this shared attitude as a healthy and strong way to enable us to continue normal life at home, at work and in our free time. Although we favour and understand this strategy, we do also think that it's a cover for the fear we feel underneath. A fear that adults want to suppress. Do adults succeed in this? Do children believe what grown-ups say or can your pretended lack of fear cause more fear for children at certain age levels? How do you then explain to a sharp seven-year-old why the media is so intensely focused on something that you and they should not fear – a non-dangerous event?

Children aren't stupid, and if you state that you're not worried at all, they'll see through this. Therefore, our explanations of adults' reactions in Part 1 of this book acknowledge that grown-ups also become frightened and worried. You yourself may even start changing your travel plans and staying away from larger crowds. When we've advocated honesty in your approach to talking about terrorism with children, it applies here too. It's much better to acknowledge your concern and explain that even though you know that the risk of terror is very small, the event makes you upset and that it's natural to be afraid. Feelings aren't always logical, and especially immediately after a terror attack you may feel scared, even though logical thoughts can tell you that the risk of this happening to you and your children is very low.

The dilemma is that through a 'stiff upper lip' attitude you may become less available and sensitive to children's expressions of threat and fear. How can you solve this dilemma? A simple answer is to allow yourself to feel and admit your fear. With kids who overtly challenge you, you can admit that you experience discomfort and fear in certain situations – big gatherings, for example – and then discuss this openly with children who are old enough. You can then explain that *risk* is something different! Everyone may feel fear, but the risk of experiencing a terrorist attack is so small that if you travelled from city to city over many years, there'd be almost no risk of being exposed to a terror event. You can explain that it's best not to think about it, but admit that sometimes you're afraid and that you try to reduce your worries by reminding yourself of the minimal risk.

This provides an opportunity to teach children about the relationship between feelings, thoughts and behaviour. Explain to them that when feelings are intense, everyone sometimes loses their grip on their thoughts and may even behave as if their fears are real. Their behaviour can be steered by their feelings, and they may, for example, stay away from a concert or a crowded place because they're afraid of terror, while there's no objective reason for this. Teach them how, when people calm down a bit, they can steer their feelings with their thoughts, and guide their behaviour differently.

PREPARE THEM FOR ACTION?

It's very difficult to prepare children for what to do if they're exposed to a terror event. Because of its rarity, we think that using time on preparation may make them more worried than necessary. It's also very difficult to know what will be the best behaviour in such events, because there are so many ways that terror can happen. That means it's really difficult to prepare children for exactly what to do in a given situation. In fact, we believe that if you teach them to respond in one way, and the specific situation demands a different response, you could possibly end up making things worse. In addition, if a child has learned by rote particular plans of what to do, it can make them be on constant guard. This creates high mental energy consumption that may interfere with their ability to concentrate and with other aspects of their life.

We'd therefore advise you to tell the children in your care to follow the instructions given by people in uniform, their teachers or other adults they see around them.

If you have a very worried child, you may have to formulate a mental plan that they can rehearse about looking for a safe place to hide, whose 'orders' they're going to follow, and the numbers they can call to get help or instruction from police or from you. Although we don't know if this will be useful in an actual situation, it can lessen the child's experience of not having any control over a situation.

With school shootings the setting is different from terror. The area it takes place is well-known. So it is possible to plan ahead. Most, if not all schools, have plans for responding to school shootings. Not because they are common, but because having a plan leads to better responses if the unlikely should happen. Through having this plan, teachers know their role; they are leaders for their students. As a parent, familiarise yourself with the school's plans for school shootings/evacuation. Know what has been communicated to your child. Keep informed and follow up on discussions at your child's school about school shootings, or when there is a lot of media attention about a shooting. If the plan is described to children at school or a drill is undertaken, follow this up at home. Reassure your child that school shootings also are rare, but they appear more common than other forms of terrorism because of the media attention they are given. Let them know that much is being done in many countries to learn more about what causes school shootings, and that this knowledge is being used to prevent them.

BUILD ON THEIR COMPASSION

When people reach out to those whose life is changed by a terror event, they show that our society has compassion. Sadness about what happened and children's compassion for families that are hurt by terror reflect how human beings care for each other. It's the exact opposite of what terrorists do when targeting innocent people. Praise children's compassion; say that it's good that they care about others. If there's something that you can do together with your children to foster this compassion – for example, placing flowers on a particular location or sending money to a fund set up for survivors and the bereaved – that may be a good symbolic act to acknowledge the victims. A conversation about how human beings care for each other may also be appropriate. Sometimes in the aftermath of a tragedy people can reflect on what's important in their lives. They can take things less for granted, value human relationships more and constructively use what has happened to re-frame their priorities.

SUMMING UP: TEN TIPS ON TALKING TO CHILDREN

Relating to recent terror attacks, we've written the following summary of ways to talk to children about terror attacks:

1. Children take in more news on disaster and terrorism than adults believe. It's important that adults talk with them and help them to understand, and do not leave them to their imaginations.

2. Be open and honest in the conversation. Be calm, but do voice the concern you as an adult have. Your own calmness will spread to your children.

3. If the children are very concerned, explain to them how tiny the risk is that the terror will affect them or you directly. Tell them that the police are being extra-vigilant.

4. Tell them that the most important thing they can do is live life normally and push away worries by doing cool things (distractions).

5. Children can practise 'strong thoughts'. If they're worried, they can repeat to themselves: 'There's no reason for this to happen here', 'The police are more alert than ever before', 'I'm safe', 'This'll be fine'.

6. Help the kids to understand. They need 'pegs' to understand what terror and terrorism are. The pegs must be simple.

7. Tell them that they can come to you at any time with their questions or concerns.

8. Show interest in what children and young people talk about among themselves. Fear is contagious and can spread in groups.

9. Be aware of how much they read or watch terrorist news. Limit their intake and talk to them about how spending a lot of time watching news can increase their fear and worry.

10. If they're very worried, ask them to set aside a daily short 'worry time' (10–15 minutes). If concerns arise outside this time, they may repeat to themselves: 'I'll think about this in my worry time.'

Further Reading

Becker-Blease, K.A., Finkelhor, D. and Turner, H. (2008) 'Media exposure predicts children's reactions to crime and terrorism.' *Journal of Trauma and Dissociation 9*, 225–248.

Comer, J.S. and Kendall, P.C. (2007) 'Terrorism: The psychological impact on youth.' *Clinical Psychology: Science and Practice 14*, 3, 179–212.

Houston, B.J., First, J., Spialek, M.L., Sorenson, M.E. and Koch, M. (2016) 'Public disaster communication and child and family disaster mental health: a review of theoretical frameworks and empirical evidence.' *Current Psychiatry Reports 18*, 54, 1–9.

Lankford, A. and Madfis, E. (2018) 'Media coverage of mass killers: content, consequences, and solutions.' *American Behavioral Scientist 62*, 2, 151–162.

Lankford, A. and Madfis, E. (2018) 'Don't name them, don't show them, but report everything else: a pragmatic proposal for denying mass killers the attention they seek and deterring future.' *American Behavioral Scientist 62*, 2, 260–279.

Otto, M.W., Henin, A., Hishrfeld-Becker, D.R., Pollack, M.H., Biederman, J. and Rosenbaum, J.F. (2007) 'Posttraumatic stress disorder symptoms following media exposure to tragic events: impact of 9/11 on children at risk for anxiety disorders.' *Journal of Anxiety Disorders 21*, 888–902.

Pfefferbaum, B., Tucker, P., Pfefferbaum, R.L., Nelson, S.D., Nitiéma, P. and Newman, E. (2018) 'Media effects in youth exposed to terrorist incidents: a historical perspective.' *Current Psychiatry Reports 20, 2*, 11.

Schonfeld, D.J., Demaria, T. and Disaster preparedness advisory council and committee on psychosocial aspects of child and family health. (2015) 'Providing psychosocial support to children and families in the aftermath of disasters and crises.' *Pediatrics 136*, 4, e1120–e1130.

Schultz, J-H., Langballe, Å. and Raundalen, M. (2014) 'Explaining the unexplainable: designing a national strategy on classroom communication concerning the 22 July attack in Norway.' *European Journal of Psychotraumatology 5*, 1.